Book 1

C Programming Success in a Day

BY SAM KEY

&

Book 2

Excel Shortcuts

BY SAM KEY

Book 1

C Programming Success in a Day

BY SAM KEY

Beginners' Guide To Fast, Easy And Efficient Learning Of C Programming

Table Contents

Introduction

I want to thank you and congratulate you for purchasing the book, "C Programming Success in a Day – Beginners guide to fast, easy and efficient learning of Cc programming".

C. is one of the most popular and most used programming languages back then and today. Many expert developers have started with learning C in order to become knowledgeable in computer programming. In some grade schools and high schools, C programming is included on their curriculum.

If you are having doubts learning the language, do not. C is actually easy to learn. Compared to C++, C is much simpler and offer little. You do not need spend years to become a master of this language.

This book will tackle the basics when it comes to C. It will cover the basic functions you need in order to create programs that can produce output and accept input. Also, in the later chapters, you will learn how to make your program capable of simple thinking. And lastly, the last chapters will deal with teaching you how to create efficient programs with the help of loops.

Anyway, before you start programming using C, you need to get some things ready. First, you will need a compiler. A compiler is a program that will translate, compile, or convert your lines of code as an executable file. It means that, you will need a compiler for you to be able to run the program you have developed.

In case you are using this book as a supplementary source of information and you are taking a course of C, you might already have a compiler given to you by your instructor. If you are not, you can get one of the compilers that are available on the internet from MinGW.org.

You will also need a text editor. One of the best text editors you can use is Notepad++. It is free and can be downloadable from the internet. Also, it works well with MinGW's compiler.

In case you do not have time to configure or install those programs, you can go and get Microsoft's Visual C++ program. It contains all the things you need in order to practice developing programs using C or C++.

The content of this book was simplified in order for you to comprehend the ideas and practices in developing programs in C easily. Thanks again for purchasing this book. I hope you enjoy it!

Chapter 1: Hello World – the Basics

When coding a C program, you must start your code with the function 'main'. By the way, a function is a collection of action that aims to achieve one or more goals. For example, a vegetable peeler has one function, which is to remove a skin of a vegetable. The peeler is composed of parts (such as the blade and handle) that will aid you to perform its function. A C function is also composed of such components and they are the lines of codes within it.

Also, take note that in order to make your coding life easier, you will need to include some prebuilt headers or functions from your compiler.

To give you an idea on what C code looks like, check the sample below:

```
#include <stdio.h>

int main()

{

        printf( "Hello World!\n" );

        getchar();

        return 0;

}
```

As you can see in the first line, the code used the #include directive to include the stdio.h in the program. In this case, the stdio.h will provide you with access to functions such as printf and getchar.

Main Declaration

After that, the second line contains int main(). This line tells the compiler that there exist a function named main. The int in the line indicates that the function main will return an integer or number.

Curly Braces

The next line contains a curly brace. In C programming, curly braces indicate the start and end of a code block or a function. A code block is a series of codes joined together in a series. When a function is called by the program, all the line of codes inside it will be executed.

Printf()

The printf function, which follows the opening curly brace is the first line of code in your main function or code block. Like the function main, the printf also have a code block within it, which is already created and included since you included <stdio.h> in your program. The function of printf is to print text into your program's display window.

Beside printf is the value or text that you want to print. It should be enclosed in parentheses to abide standard practice. The value that the code want to print is Hello World!. To make sure that printf to recognize that you want to print a string and display the text properly, it should be enclosed inside double quotation marks.

By the way, in programming, a single character is called a character while a sequence of characters is called a string.

Escape Sequence

You might have noticed that the sentence is followed by a \n. In C, \n means new line. Since your program will have problems if you put a new line or press enter on the value of the printf, it is best to use its text equivalent or the escape sequence of the new line.

By the way, the most common escape sequences used in C are:

\t = tab

\f = new page

\r = carriage return

\b = backspace

\v = vertical tab

Semicolons

After the last parenthesis, a semicolon follows. And if you look closer, almost every line of code ends with it. The reasoning behind that is that the semicolon acts as an indicator that it is the end of the line of code or command. Without it, the compiler will think that the following lines are included in the printf function. And if that happens, you will get a syntax error.

Getchar()

Next is the getchar() function. Its purpose is to receive user input from the keyboard. Many programmers use it as a method on pausing a program and letting the program wait for the user to interact with it before it executes the next line of code. To make the program move through after the getchar() function, the user must press the enter key.

In the example, if you compile or run it without getchar(), the program will open the display or the console, display the text, and then immediately close. Without the break provided by the getchar() function, the computer will execute those commands instantaneously. And the program will open and close so fast that you will not be able to even see the Hello World text in the display.

Return Statement

The last line of code in the function is return 0. The return statement is essential in function blocks. When the program reaches this part, the return statement will tell the program its value. Returning the 0 value will make the program interpret that the function or code block that was executed successfully.

And at the last line of the example is the closing curly brace. It signifies that the program has reached the end of the function.

It was not that not hard, was it? With that example alone, you can create simple programs that can display text. Play around with it a bit and familiarize yourself with C's basic syntax.

Chapter 2: Basic Input Output

After experimenting with what you learned in the previous chapter, you might have realized that it was not enough. It was boring. And just displaying what you typed in your program is a bit useless.

This time, this chapter will teach you how to create a program that can interact with the user. Check this code example:

```
#include <stdio.h>

int main()

{

        int number_container;

        printf( "Enter any number you want! " );

        scanf( “%d”, &number_container );

        printf( "The number you entered is %d”, number_container );

        getchar();

        return 0;

}
```

Variables

You might have noticed the int number_container part in the first line of the code block. int number_container is an example of variable declaration. To declare a variable in C, you must indicate the variable type first, and then the name of the variable name.

In the example, int was indicated as the variable or data type, which means the variable is an integer. There are other variable types in C such as float for floating-point numbers, char for characters, etc. Alternatively, the name number_container was indicated as the variable's name or identifier.

Variables are used to hold values throughout the program and code blocks. The programmer can let them assign a value to it and retrieve its value when it is needed.

For example:

```
int number_container;

number_container = 3;

printf ( "The variables value is %d", number_container );
```

In that example, the first line declared that the program should create an integer variable named number_container. The second line assigned a value to the variable. And the third line makes the program print the text together with the value of the variable. When executed, the program will display:

```
The variables value is 3
```

You might have noticed the %d on the printf line on the example. The %d part indicates that the next value that will be printed will be an integer. Also, the quotation on the printf ended after %d. Why is that?

In order to print the value of a variable, it must be indicated with the double quotes. If you place double quotes on the variables name, the compiler will treat it as a literal string. If you do this:

```
int number_container;
```

```
number_container = 3;

printf ( "The variables value is number_container" );
```

The program will display:

```
The variables value is number_container
```

By the way, you can also use %i as a replacement for %d.

Assigning a value to a variable is simple. Just like in the previous example, just indicate the name of variable, follow it with an equal sign, and declare its value.

When creating variables, you must make sure that each variable will have unique names. Also, the variables should never have the same name as functions. In addition, you can declare multiple variables in one line by using commas. Below is an example:

```
int first_variable, second_variable, third_variable;
```

Those three variables will be int type variables. And again, never forget to place a semicolon after your declaration.

When assigning a value or retrieving the value of a variable, make sure that you declare its existence first. If not, the compiler will return an error since it will try to access something that does not exist yet.

Scanf()

In the first example in this chapter, you might have noticed the scanf function. The scanf function is also included in the <stdio.h>. Its purpose is to retrieve text user input from the user.

After the program displays the 'Enter any number you want' text, it will proceed in retrieving a number from the user. The cursor will be appear after the text since the new line escape character was no included in the printf.

The cursor will just blink and wait for the user to enter any characters or numbers. To let the program get the number the user typed and let it proceed to the next line of code, he must press the Enter key. Once he does that, the program will display the text 'The number you entered is' and the value of the number the user inputted a while ago.

To make the scanf function work, you must indicate the data type it needs to receive and the location of the variable where the value that scanf will get will be stored. In the example:

```
scanf( "%d", &number_container );
```

The first part "%d" indicates that the scanf function must retrieve an integer. On the other hand, the next part indicates the location of the variable. You must have noticed the ampersand placed in front of the variable's name. The ampersand retrieves the location of the variable and tells it to the function.

Unlike the typical variable value assignment, scanf needs the location of the variable instead of its name alone. Due to that, without the ampersand, the function will not work.

Math or Arithmetic Operators

Aside from simply giving number variables with values by typing a number, you can assign values by using math operators. In C, you can add, subtract, multiply, and divide numbers and assign the result to variables directly. For example:

```
int sum;

sum = 1 + 2;
```

If you print the value of sum, it will return a 3, which is the result of the addition of 1 and 2. By the way, the + sign is for addition, - for subtraction, * for multiplication, and / for division.

With the things you have learned as of now, you can create a simple calculator program. Below is an example code:

```
#include <stdio.h>

int main()

{

        int first_addend, second_addend, sum;

        printf( "Enter the first addend! " );

        scanf( “%d”, &first_addend );

        printf( "\nEnter the second addend! " );

        scanf( “%d”, &second_addend );

        sum = first_addend + second_addend;

        printf( "The sum of the two numbers is %d”, sum );

        getchar();

        return 0;

}
```

Chapter 3: Conditional Statements

The calculator program seems nice, is it not? However, the previous example limits you on creating programs that only uses one operation, which is a bit disappointing. Well, in this chapter, you can improve that program with the help of if or conditional statements. And of course, learning this will improve your overall programming skills. This is the part where you will be able to make your program 'think'.

'If' statements can allow you to create branches in your code blocks. Using them allows you to let the program think and perform specific functions or actions depending on certain variables and situations. Below is an example:

```
#include <stdio.h>

int main()

{

        int some_number;

        printf( “Welcome to Guess the Magic Number program. \n” );

        printf( “Guess the magic number to win. \n” );

        printf( "Type the magic number and press Enter: " );

        scanf( “%d”, &some_number );

        if ( some_number == 3 ) {

                printf( "You guessed the right number! " );

        }

        getchar();

        return 0;

}
```

In the example, the if statement checked if the value of the variable some_number is equal to number 3. In case the user entered the number 3 on the program, the comparison between the variable some_number and three will return TRUE since the value of some_number 3 is true. Since the value that the if statement received was TRUE, then it will process the code block below it. And the result will be:

You guessed the right number!

If the user input a number other than three, the comparison will return a FALSE value. If that happens, the program will skip the code block in the if statement and proceed to the next line of code after the if statement's code block.

By the way, remember that you need to use the curly braces to enclosed the functions that you want to happen in case your if statement returns TRUE. Also, when inserting if statement, you do not need to place a semicolon after the if statement or its code block's closing curly brace. However, you will still need to place semicolons on the functions inside the code blocks of your if statements.

TRUE and FALSE

The if statement will always return TRUE if the condition is satisfied. For example, the condition in the if statement is 10 > 2. Since 10 is greater than 2, then it is true. On the other hand, the if statement will always return FALSE if the condition is not satisfied. For example, the condition in the if statement is 5 < 5. Since 5 is not less than 5, then the statement will return a FALSE.

Note that if statements only return two results: TRUE and FALSE. In computer programming, the number equivalent to TRUE is any nonzero number. In some cases, it is only the number 1. On the other hand, the number equivalent of FALSE is zero.

Operators

Also, if statements use comparison, Boolean, or relational and logical operators. Some of those operators are:

== – equal to

!= – not equal to

> – greater than

< – less than

>= – greater than or equal to

<= – less than or equal to

Else Statement

There will be times that you would want your program to do something else in case your if statement return FALSE. And that is what the else statement is for. Check the example below:

```
#include <stdio.h>

int main()

{

        int some_number;

        printf( “Welcome to Guess the Magic Number program. \n” );

        printf( “Guess the magic number to win. \n” );

        printf( "Type the magic number and press Enter: " );

        scanf( “%d”, &some_number );

        if ( some_number == 3 ) {

                printf( "You guessed the right number! " );
```

```
    }
    else {
        printf( "Sorry. That is the wrong number" );
    }
    getchar();
    return 0;
}
```

If ever the if statement returns FALSE, the program will skip next to the else statement immediately. And since the if statement returns FALSE, it will immediately process the code block inside the else statement.

For example, if the number the user inputted on the program is 2, the if statement will return a FALSE. Due to that, the else statement will be processed, and the program will display:

```
Sorry. That is the wrong number
```

On the other hand, if the if statement returns TRUE, it will process the if statement's code block, but it will bypass all the succeeding else statements below it.

Else If

If you want more conditional checks on your program, you will need to take advantage of else if. Else if is a combination of the if and else statement. It will act like an else statement, but instead of letting the program execute the code block below it, it will perform another check as if it was an if statement. Below is an example:

```
#include <stdio.h>

int main()

{

    int some_number;

    printf( “Welcome to Guess the Magic Number program. \n” );

    printf( “Guess the magic number to win. \n” );

    printf( "Type the magic number and press Enter: " );

    scanf( “%d”, &some_number );

    if ( some_number == 3 ) {

        printf( "You guessed the right number! " );

    }

    else if ( some_number > 3 ){

        printf( "Your guess is too high!" );

    }

    else {

        printf( "Your guess is too low!" );

    }

    getchar();

    return 0;

}
```

In case the if statement returns FALSE, the program will evaluate the else if statement. If it returns TRUE, it will execute its code block and ignore the following else statements. However, if it is FALSE, it will proceed on the last else statement, and execute its code block. And just like before, if the first if statement returns true, it will disregard the following else and else if statements.

In the example, if the user inputs 3, he will get the You guessed the right number message. If the user inputs 4 or higher, he will get the Your guess is too high message. And if he inputs any other number, he will get a Your guess is too low message since any number aside from 3 and 4 or higher is automatically lower than 3.

With the knowledge you have now, you can upgrade the example calculator program to handle different operations. Look at the example and study it:

```
#include <stdio.h>

int main()

{

        int first_number, second_number, result, operation;

        printf( "Enter the first number: " );

        scanf( “%d”, &first_number );

        printf( "\nEnter the second number: " );

        scanf( “%d”, &second_number );

        printf ( “What operation would you like to use? \n” );

        printf ( “Enter 1 for addition. \n” );

        printf ( “Enter 2 for subtraction. \n” );

        printf ( “Enter 3 for multiplication. \n” );

        printf ( “Enter 4 for division. \n” );
```

```
    scanf( "%d", &operation );
    if ( operation == 1 ) {
        result = first_number + second_number;
        printf( "The sum is %d", result );
    }
    else if ( operation == 2 ){
        result = first_number - second_number;
        printf( "The difference is %d", result );
    }
    else if ( operation == 3 ){
        result = first_number * second_number;
        printf( "The product is %d", result );
    }
    else if ( operation == 4 ){
        result = first_number / second_number;
        printf( "The quotient is %d", result );
    }
    else {
        printf( "You have entered an invalid choice." );
    }
    getchar();
    return 0;
}
```

Chapter 4: Looping in C

The calculator's code is getting better, right? As of now, it is possible that you are thinking about the programs that you could create with the usage of the conditional statements.

However, as you might have noticed in the calculator program, it seems kind of painstaking to use. You get to only choose one operation every time you run the program. When the calculation ends, the program closes. And that can be very annoying and unproductive.

To solve that, you must create loops in the program. Loops are designed to let the program execute some of the functions inside its code blocks. It effectively eliminates the need to write some same line of codes. It saves the time of the programmer and it makes the program run more efficiently.

There are four different ways in creating a loop in C. In this chapter, two of the only used and simplest loop method will be discussed. To grasp the concept of looping faster, check the example below:

```
#include <stdio.h>
int main()
{
        int some_number;
        int guess_result;
        guess_result = 0;

        printf( "Welcome to Guess the Magic Number program. \n" );
        printf( "Guess the magic number to win. \n" );
        printf( "You have unlimited chances to guess the number. \n" );
```

```
    while ( guess_result == 0 ) {

        printf( "Guess the magic number: " );
        scanf( “%d”, &some_number );
        if ( some_number == 3 ) {
            printf( "You guessed the right number! \n" );
            guess_result = 1;
        }
        else if ( some_number > 3 ){
            printf( "Your guess is too high! \n" );
            guess_result = 0;
        }
        else {
            printf( "Your guess is too low! \n" );
            guess_result = 0;
        }
    }
    printf( "Thank you for playing. Press Enter to exit this program." );
    getchar();
    return 0;
}
```

While Loop

In this example, the while loop function was used. The while loop allows the program to execute the code block inside it as long as the condition is met or the argument in it returns TRUE. It is one of the simplest loop function in C. In the example, the condition that the while loop requires is that the guess_result variable should be equal to 0.

As you can see, in order to make sure that the while loop will start, the value of the guess_result variable was set to 0.

If you have not noticed it yet, you can actually nest code blocks within code blocks. In this case, the code block of the if and else statements were inside the code block of the while statement.

Anyway, every time the code reaches the end of the while statement and the guess_result variable is set to 0, it will repeat itself. And to make sure that the program or user experience getting stuck into an infinite loop, a safety measure was included.

In the example, the only way to escape the loop is to guess the magic number. If the if statement within the while code block was satisfied, its code block will run. In that code block, a line of code sets the variable guess_result's value to 1. This effectively prevent the while loop from running once more since the guess_result's value is not 0 anymore, which makes the statement return a FALSE.

Once that happens, the code block of the while loop and the code blocks inside it will be ignored. It will skip to the last printf line, which will display the end program message 'Thank you for playing. Press Enter to exit this program'.

For Loop

The for loop is one of the most handy looping function in C. And its main use is to perform repetitive commands on a set number of times. Below is an example of its use:

```
#include <stdio.h>

int main()

{

    int some_number;

    int x;

    int y;


    printf( "Welcome to Guess the Magic Number program. \n" );

    printf( "Guess the magic number to win. \n" );

    printf( "You have only three chance of guessing. \n" );

    printf( "If you do not get the correct answer after guessing three times. \n"
    );

    printf( "This program will be terminated. \n" );


    for (x = 0; x < 3; x++) {

        y = 3 – x;

        printf( "The number of guesses that you have left is: %d", y );

        printf( "\nGuess the magic number: " );

        scanf( "%d", &some_number );

        if ( some_number == 3 ) {

            printf( "You guessed the right number! \n" );

            x = 4;

        }

        else if ( some_number > 3 ){
```

```
                printf( "Your guess is too high! \n " );
            }
            else {
                printf( "Your guess is too low! \n " );
            }
        }
        printf( "Press the Enter button to close this program. \n" );
        getchar();
        getchar();
        return 0;
}
```

The for statement's argument section or part requires three things. First, the initial value of the variable that will be used. In this case, the example declared that x = 0. Second, the condition. In the example, the for loop will run until x has a value lower than 3. Third, the variable update line. Every time the for loop loops, the variable update will be executed. In this case, the variable update that will be triggered is x++.

Increment and Decrement Operators

By the way, x++ is a variable assignment line. The x is the variable and the ++ is an increment operator. The function of an increment operator is to add 1 to the variable where it was placed. In this case, every time the program reads x++, the program will add 1 to the variable x. If x has a value of 10, the increment operator will change variable x's value to 11.

On the other hand, you can also use the decrement operator instead of the increment operator. The decrement operator is done by place -- next to a variable. Unlike the increment operator, the decrement subtracts 1 to its operand.

Just like the while loop, the for loop will run as long as its condition returns TRUE. However, the for loop has a built in safety measure and variable declaration. You do not need to declare the value needed for its condition outside the statement. And the safety measure to prevent infinite loop is the variable update. However, it does not mean that it will be automatically immune to infinite loops. Poor programming can lead to it. For example:

```
for (x = 1; x > 1; x++) {

        /* Insert Code Block Here */

}
```

In this example, the for loop will enter into an infinite loop unless a proper means of escape from the loop is coded inside its code block.

The structure of the for loop example is almost the same with while loop. The only difference is that the program is set to loop for only three times. In this case, it only allows the user to guess three times or until the value of variable x does not reach 3 or higher.

Every time the user guesses wrong, the value of x is incremented, which puts the loop closer in ending. However, in case the user guesses right, the code block of the if statement assigns a value higher than 3 to variable x in order to escape the loop and end the program.

Conclusion

Thank you again for purchasing this book!

I hope this book was able to help you to learn the basics of C programming. The next step is to learn the other looping methods, pointers, arrays, strings, command line arguments, recursion, and binary trees.

Finally, if you enjoyed this book, please take the time to share your thoughts and post a review on Amazon. We do our best to reach out to readers and provide the best value we can. Your positive review will help us achieve that. It'd be greatly appreciated!
Thank you and good luck!

Book 2

Excel Shortcuts

BY SAM KEY

The 100 Top Best Powerful Excel Keyboard Shortcuts in 1 Day!

Table Of Contents

Introduction

I want to thank you and congratulate you for purchasing the book, "The Power of Excel Shortcuts: The 100 Top Best Powerful Excel Keyboard Shortcuts in 1 Day!". This book contains proven steps and strategies on how to master the Microsoft Excel through just 100 keyboard shortcuts! However, most people will ask, "Why do you need to learn these shortcuts anyway?"

Advantages of Using Microsoft Excel

Microsoft Excel has become one of the most commonly used enterprise software in schools and offices. Its way of presenting data, which is through a spreadsheet, has helped a lot of people especially in the field of data mining. If you were going to put numerous rows of data, in let's say, a word processing program, it might take a lot of time creating tables and formatting each of them to fit in the pages. With the Microsoft Excel, these manual tasks are now much easier.

What does the Microsoft Excel have that other programs don't? For one, it has a built-in spreadsheet that you can manipulate the size and formatting. This versatile way of maneuvering the spreadsheet made it indispensable for many. Now, gone are the days were people have to manually draw tables in sheets of paper. Excel has already the tables prepared for them.

Another nifty feature of this software is its calculation function. Excel houses a myriad of formulas for solving arithmetic, financial and logical problems, among others. Thus, one doesn't even need to calculate every sum or average of a data series. Just by using a formula in Excel, everything can be done in an instant.

The Secret behind Mastering Excel

Speaking of instant, did you know that Excel has more than a hundred keyboard shortcuts? What does this mean to you as an Excel user? It means you can continuously work on your Excel spreadsheet without having to depend on your mouse constantly for Excel functions.

This is especially helpful whenever you are inputting a lot of data, and doing this will be more efficient if both of your hands weren't switching from keyboard to mouse and vice versa, every once in a while. In addition, if your mouse suddenly chose the most inopportune time to malfunction, learning Excel shortcuts can save you from major headaches.

As such, this book will provide you 100 keyboard shortcuts which you can use in Excel. In addition, as a bonus, you will learn about alternatives in case you forget any of these shortcuts.

Thanks again for purchasing this book, I hope you enjoy it!

Chapter 1: Moving Around the Excel Screen

People typically use the mouse for navigating the Excel screen. With this device, you can manipulate every cell in Excel, including its formatting and color. Since the mouse can access the major functions in Excel through the ribbon, there is no need for you to manually-type every formula or command.
However, the only difficult thing that you cannot do with a mouse is entering text. If you're going to use an on-screen keyboard, keying in the data in every cell would probably take you a lot longer than just using the keyboard for the text.
Thus, if you're going to use the keyboard most of the time, especially if you're just starting to build the spreadsheet data from scratch, it would be helpful to learn the basic keyboard shortcuts for moving around the Excel spreadsheet.

Shortcut #1: Arrow Keys
There are four arrow keys found in the right side of your main keyboard keys. These are the Arrow Left, Arrow Right, Arrow Up, and Arrow Down keys. Intuitively, you know that you can use these keys for moving within the spreadsheet. For instance, by selecting a cell then pressing Arrow Up, it will situate the cursor in the cell directly above your selected cell.

Shortcut #2: Ctrl + Arrow Key
Let's assume that you have a block of Excel data that spans more than 50,000 rows and more than 200 columns. You would probably have a hard time using a mouse in skimming these voluminous data. As such, you can use the Ctrl + Arrow key to navigate each "ends" of the data easily. In this example, click any cell in the block of data then press Ctrl + Arrow Down. You will be immediately located to the bottom cell in that specific column.

Shortcut #3: Shift + Arrow Key
You have selected all the items in the row but you forgot to include one cell. What would you do if you needed to include the next cell in the selection? Simply press Shift + Arrow Key, where the arrow pertains to the direction of the region you want to highlight.

Shortcut #4: Ctrl + Shift + Arrow Key
The above shortcut only includes one cell in the selection; but what would happen if you want to include everything until the last cell containing a data? You then use the Ctrl + Shift + Arrow Key.

Shortcut #5: Backspace
The Backspace key immediately deletes the contents of the active cell. However, if the cell is in Edit mode, it will only delete one character in the left of the insertion point, or the blinking cursor in the Formula bar.

Shortcut #6: Delete

This key has the same function as the Backspace key. However, instead of the left side, it removes a character in the right hand side of the insertion point.

Shortcut #7: End
Pressing the End key will enable the End Mode in Excel. In this mode, if you press an Arrow key, it will directly take you to the last used cell (or if none, last cell) in that specific direction. However, if the Scroll Lock is on, pressing the End key will only take you to the lower right corner of your Excel screen.

Shortcut #8: Ctrl + End
It works the same as the End key where pressing this combination will take you to the last used cell. However, if no cells were used, it will not move to the end of the worksheet like the End key does. Also, if the insertion point is located in the Formula bar (e.g., after the first character), Ctrl + End will put this cursor at the end of the field.

Shortcut #9: Ctrl + Shift + End
This keyboard shortcut can do two functions. First, in the Formula bar, it will select every character at the right of the insertion point. On the other hand, if you use it in the worksheet, it will highlight the cells starting from the active cell (or selected cell) until the last used cell in the worksheet.

Shortcut #10: Spacebar
Aside from putting a space in your text, it can also either select or clear a checkbox.

Shortcut #11: Ctrl + Spacebar
This will select the whole column to where the active cell is located.

Shortcut #12: Shift + Spacebar
It has the same function as the above, but this shortcut selects rows instead of columns.

Shortcut #13: Ctrl + Shift + Spacebar
Pressing these keys will select your entire worksheet.

Shortcut #14: Enter
After you have entered a data in a cell, pressing the Enter key will complete the input of data. Besides that, you can also directly go one cell below through this key. Considered as the most commonly used shortcut in Excel, you will be using the Enter key quite a lot because all Excel functions need it.

Shortcut #15: Shift + Enter
If you press Enter, you will go down one cell. Conversely, a Shift + Enter will complete an entry in a cell but the cursor will go directly above your entry.

Shortcut #16: Ctrl + Enter

Since this is a spreadsheet, it follows that after you have put an entry, you will enter another data below it. That is the common task whenever you're working on a table or database, which explains why the Enter key goes down. However, if you think that you need the downward movement, you can try Ctrl + Enter. This will plainly enter your data in the cell and it won't move your cursor to another direction.

Shortcut #17: Alt + Enter
You want the data to go into the next line in the same cell. However, if you press Enter, the cursor just moves on to the next cell in line. Pressing the Tab key doesn't work either. So what will you do? Try Alt + Enter key and see if it works.

Shortcut #18: Esc Key
The Escape key, or simply "Esc", performs a lot of nifty functions in Excel. Among of which are the following: 1) deletes a whole data in a cell, 2) exits you from a dialog box, and 3) escapes you from the full screen mode of Excel.

Shortcut #19: Home Key
The Home key will take you to the first cell in the specific row of your active cell. However, if the Scroll Lock is on, the cursor will go to the upper-left corner of your current window.

Shortcut #20: Ctrl + Home
This shortcut, also known as the "True Home key", brings the user to the beginning of the worksheet.

Shortcut #21: Ctrl + Shift + Home
This will select all cells from the active cell up to the first cell in the worksheet.

Shortcut #22: Page Down
Scouring among rows and rows of worksheets is now easy because of this button. This will display the next page in your Excel window.

Shortcut #23: Alt + Page Down
Unlike Page Down, the Alt + Page Down combination will show the next page to the right of your current window.

Shortcut #24: Ctrl + Page Down
Flipping in several worksheets is now easy thanks to Ctrl + Page Down. This will automatically turn you over to the next worksheet.

Shortcut #25: Ctrl + Shift + Page Down
The normal way of selecting several worksheets at once is to hold Ctrl while clicking each of the worksheets to be included in the selection. However, for those who don't think this is the practical way to do it, here's an alternative. Use the Ctrl + Shift + Page Down; it will automatically select the sheets for you.

Shortcut #26: Page Up
This is quite similar to Shortcut #22: Page Down key, except for the fact that this one goes in the opposite direction (which is upward).

Shortcut #27: Alt + Page Up
The Alt + Page Up will move your screen to the left, instead of right as what was described in Shortcut #23: Alt + Page Down.

Shortcut #28: Ctrl + Page Up
Same as Shortcut #24: Ctrl + Page Down, this will enable you to change sheets easily. However, this one goes in a counterclockwise direction.

Shortcut #29: Ctrl + Shift + Page Up
Selecting sheets is also a function of the Ctrl + Shift + Page Up. However, it will select the worksheets on the left hand side of your current sheet first.

Shortcut #30: Tab Key
Using the Tab key will enable you to move to the right hand side of the cell. Also, if you have a protected worksheet, pressing this can immediately take you to the next unlocked cell. Lastly, in case there is a dialog box, you can easily move along the options through the Tab key.

Shortcut #31: Shift + Tab
The Shift + Tab works the opposite way; if pressing Tab will take you to the right hand cell, this shortcut will locate the left cell for you. It also applies to the other functions of the Tab key. In a dialog box for instance, keying in Shift + Tab will move you to the previous option.

Shortcut #32: Ctrl + Tab
You're now done with shortcuts for moving around cells and worksheets. As such, the succeeding shortcuts in this chapter will focus on dialog boxes. For this shortcut, use it if you want to go to the next tab in a dialog box.

Shortcut #33: Ctrl + Shift + Tab
However, if you wish to go back to the previous tab in a dialog box, using the Ctrl + Shift + Tab is the right combination.

So there you have it, the first 33 keyboard shortcuts in Excel. Hopefully, through these tips you can know traverse in your multitude of cells and worksheets with no difficulty at all.

Chapter 2: Navigating the Excel Ribbon

Microsoft created the "ribbon" as a replacement to the expanding menus in the earlier versions of Microsoft Excel. It houses all the functions in Excel such as formatting, page layout, pictures, and shapes. However, since its interface is not in an expanding menu style, people are not that familiar with its keyboard shortcuts as compared to before where you can immediately see which shortcut runs which.
To help you with that, here are some of the most commonly used keyboard shortcuts for exploring the Ribbon.

Shortcut #34: Alt Key
Letters and numbers will appear in the ribbon once you push the Alt key. What happens is that it activates the access keys, wherein typing in corresponding letter or number will let you select a specific function in the ribbon.

Shortcut #35: F10
This key has the same function as the Alt key, only that pressing the F10 would require you to use your right hand instead.

Shortcut #36: Alt + Arrow Left/Right
To be able to navigate to the other tabs, use these keys.

Shortcut #37: F10 + Arrow Left/Right
Since it was previously mentioned that the F10 behaves the same way as the Alt key, pressing F10 followed by an arrow to the left or to the right will also transfer you to other tabs.

Shortcut #38: Ctrl + F1
There's no doubt that the ribbon indeed takes up quite a lot of space in your screen. Therefore, for those who want more area for their spreadsheet, hiding the ribbon is the best option. To do that, simply press Ctrl + F1. To show the ribbon again, also press the same shortcut.

Shortcut #39: Shift + F10
Shift + F10 is similar to the right click button of your mouse. It can open menus and other options depending on where your cursor is.

Shortcut #40: F6
You can move along three areas of the screen through this key. The F6 key, will take you either to the ribbon, the spreadsheet, or the status bar.

Shortcut #41: F10 + Tab
In a tab, you can browse through the functions by pressing this combination continuously. You can also press this shortcut first, and then proceed with the arrow keys for navigation.

Shortcut #42: F10 + Shift + Tab
The above shortcut goes around the functions in a clockwise manner. On the contrary, the F10 + Shift + Tab shortcut does otherwise.

Shortcut #43: F1
In the upper right corner of the ribbon, there is a blue question mark icon. Accessing this icon will take you to the Microsoft Excel Help task pane. Alternatively, if you press F1 the same pane will open.

Since the area around the ribbon is limited, it is only appropriate that there would be less keyboard shortcuts dedicated for it. All in all, there are ten button combinations for the ribbon.

Chapter 3: Formatting the Excel Spreadsheet

If you're also a user of the Microsoft Word, you are probably familiar with formatting keyboard shortcuts such as Ctrl + B, which stands for bold text or Ctrl + I, which italicizes your text. Since you can do almost every basic feature that you need in the Word application through the keyboard, this makes the formatting easier for you.
Fortunately, even though Excel is not a word-processing program, it also has dedicated keyboard shortcuts that for formatting. These are as follows:

Shortcut #44: Alt + '
By going to the Styles group in the Home tab, you can quickly change the appearance of the cell by selecting any of the pre-installed styles in Excel. To see the formatting changes done within a cell, you click on the New Style option, which will take you to the Style dialog box. Similarly, clicking Alt + ' will get you in the same menu.

Shortcut #45: Ctrl + B
Like in Microsoft Word, Ctrl + B will either apply or remove a bold format in a text.

Shortcut #46: Ctrl + 2
This shortcut can also make the selected text into a bold type.

Shortcut #47: Ctrl + I
Letter I stands for Italics. As such, clicking Ctrl + I will turn any text into an italicized type.

Shortcut #48: Ctrl + 3
This also functions like the Ctrl + I shortcut.

Shortcut #49: Ctrl + U
Ctrl + U will put an underline in the selected text.

Shortcut #50: Ctrl + 4
Another alternative for the Ctrl +U is the Ctrl + 4 shortcut.

Shortcut #51: Ctrl + 5
To easily put a strikethrough in your text, press Ctrl + 5.

Shortcut #52: Ctrl + Shift + F
If you want more font formatting options, you can just proceed to the Font tab of the Format cells dialog box. Right-clicking a cell then selecting Format Cells will get you there, or you can just use this shortcut.

Shortcut #53: Ctrl + Shift + P

This shortcut works the same as the above.

Shortcut #54: Ctrl + Shift + &
Now that you're done with editing the text, this shortcut as well as the succeeding ones will pertain to cell formatting. As for Ctrl + Shift + &, it will put a plain black border on all sides of the cell.

Shortcut #55: Ctrl + Shift + _
On the contrary, Ctrl + Shift + _ will remove the borders that you have made.

Shortcut #56: F4
Instead of manually doing all the formatting for a number of cells, Excel has a shortcut wherein you can redo the formatting that you just did in another cell. This is the F4 function key. For example, if you have put borders in Cell A1, selecting Cell A2 then pressing F4 will also create borders for that specific cell.

Shortcut #57: Ctrl + 1
Pressing the Ctrl + 1 will show the Format Cells dialog box. In this box, you can edit every possible formatting for a cell such as number format, alignment, font, border, and fill.

The previous chapters have discussed how certain shortcuts can perform specific functions in Excel such as formatting cells and navigating the spreadsheet. In the following chapters, the topics will be about the different uses of specific buttons such as the Function keys and the Control key.

Chapter 4: Working with Function Keys

The first row of keys in your keyboard contains the function keys, which is denoted by the letter F followed by a number. In the Windows desktop, these function keys can do a variety of tasks such as adjusting the screen brightness or minimizing the volume.
Excel uses the function keys for different purposes. Thus, most people usually have a difficulty mastering the Function key shortcuts in Excel.

Shortcut #58: Alt + F1
Alt + F1 will automatically create a chart for you. Just select the range of cells containing your chart data then press this shortcut. Afterwards, a column chart will appear in the worksheet.

Shortcut #59: Alt + Shift + F1
The normal way in creating a new worksheet is by right-clicking any of the existing worksheets then choosing Insert. The same task can be done by this shortcut.

Shortcut #60: F2
In editing a formula, you can't just simply select an active cell; you have to click on the Formula bar so that you can make changes to it. Fortunately, the F2 will put the cell in Edit mode. Thus, if you want to amend a cell, there's no need for you to click on the Formula bar; just use F2 instead.

Shortcut #61: Shift + F2
The Shift + F2 shortcut will insert comments in the active cell.

Shortcut #62: Ctrl + F2
Unlike the previous F2 combinations, this one has nothing to do with editing a cell. When you press Ctrl + F2, you will be forwarded to the Print Preview screen. Upon exiting this screen, your spreadsheet will show dotted lines which serves as a marker for a page border.

Shortcut #63: F3
Instead of constantly referring to a range of cells by their cell location (e.g., A1:D1), you can just define a name for this range. Thus, whenever you want to pertain to that specific range in a formula, you can simply put its name; there's no need for you to put the cell range. F3 will take you to the Paste Name dialog box, wherein you can list all the names created in a worksheet and their respective cell references.

Shortcut #64: Ctrl + F3
To create a new name, go to the Name Manager through Ctrl + F3.

Shortcut #65: Shift + F3

Using formulas is the heart of Microsoft Excel. Without it, you cannot do any calculations in the spreadsheet. As such, there is a dedicated tab for Formulas in the Excel ribbon. However, it may take quite a lot of time for users to efficiently look for the appropriate formula with all the possible options in the Formulas tab. Because of this, the Shift + F3 key combination is made. It opens the Insert Function dialog box, wherein you can easily search for a formula by just typing in the description of what you need to do.

Shortcut #66: Ctrl + F4
You don't need to click that "X" mark in the upper left corner of your Excel screen just to close the application; a simple Ctrl + F4 is enough to do the job.

Shortcut #67: F5
Rummaging through a lot of cells takes a lot of work, especially if you're dealing with thousands of rows in a spreadsheet. The Go To dialog box, which can be accessed through F5, will help you reach that specific cell or range that you wanted to see.

Shortcut #68: Ctrl + F5
By default, all workbooks are always in full screen mode in Excel. However, if you're doing work on several Excel files at once, it may be hard to switch from one file to the other when each workbook is on full screen. Through Ctrl + F5, the selected file restore to window size in the Excel screen so that you can easily switch across files.

Shortcut #69: Shift + F6
This works the same as Shortcut #40: F6, albeit in a counterclockwise direction.

Shortcut #70: Ctrl + F6
If you have more than one workbook open, pressing Ctrl + F6 will let you switch among these workbooks.

Shortcut #71: F7
Aside from Microsoft Word, the Excel application has also a built-in spell checker. To check the spelling of every word in your spreadsheet, press F7. This will run the Spelling dialog box. Apart from detecting erroneous spellings, it also suggests possible words that can replace the incorrect word.

Shortcut #72: Ctrl + F7
As mentioned before, you should not use the full screen mode when working with several Excel files. This is so that you can select each workbook with ease. The Ctrl + F7 shortcut executes the Move command so that you can drag the unneeded workbooks in another area in the Excel screen where it can't obstruct your view.

Shortcut #73: F8

Upon pressing F8, the Excel goes into an Extend Selection mode. This enables you to use the arrow keys to extend the current selection. Pressing the same key will also lift the Extend Selection mode.

Shortcut #74: Shift + F8
The limitation of the F8 key is that it only adds adjacent cells in the selection. Through Shift + F8, you can now add any nonadjacent cell by using arrow keys.

Shortcut #75: Ctrl + F8
To resize your workbook, use Ctrl + F8. This will run the Size command for workbooks that are not in a full screen mode.

Shortcut #76: Alt + F8
A macro is a set of actions created using the Visual Basic programming language. What it does is to automate a set of tasks in Excel. For example, you're going to retrieve a data in a one sheet then you'll paste the said data in another sheet. However, if you're going to do the copy-paste task for thousands of data, it might take you a long time. As such, you can use the macro for this. Alt + F8 will open the Macro dialog box, where you can record and run a macro.

Shortcut #77: F9
This is the Refresh button in Excel. Once you refresh a workbook, it will recalculate all new formulas in the said file.

Shortcut #78: Shift + F9
On the other hand, Shift + F9 will only recalculate the formulas in the worksheet you are currently working on.

Shortcut #79: Ctrl + Alt + F9
This has the same function as F9, but it will also recalculate formulas that have not been changed.

Shortcut #80: Ctrl + Alt + Shift + F9
Aside from doing what the Ctrl + Alt + F9 shortcut does, it also rechecks all dependent formulas for any errors.

Shortcut #81: Alt + Shift + F10
Smart tags are data that are labeled in a particular type. For instance, a person's name in an Outlook email message can be labeled with this tag. You can open the smart tag menu through this shortcut.

Shortcut #82: Ctrl + F10
This will enable a workbook to display in full screen mode (or maximized mode).

Shortcut #83: F11
The Shortcut #58: Alt + F1 will let you create charts by highlighting the data series. Similarly, the F11 key has the same function except that you don't need to

select the data series; it will automatically detect the data for you. Another difference between these two shortcuts is that the Alt + F1 will display the chart in the same worksheet, while the F1 key will make another worksheet for the new chart.

Shortcut #84: Shift + F11
This is an alternative to Shortcut #59: Alt + Shift + F1, wherein it will insert a new worksheet.

Shortcut #85: Alt + F11
Alt + F11 will open the Microsoft Visual Basic Editor. In this menu, you can create or edit a macro by using the Visual Basic for Applications (VBA) programming language.

Shortcut #86: F12
The F12 key is the shortcut for the Save As dialog box. It lets you save your Excel file among the available formats.

In case you're wondering why the F1, F4, F6 and F10 keys as well as some of their derivatives are not included in the list, these function keys have already been discussed in the previous chapters. Moreover, as this book specifically claims that it will contain at least a hundred keyboard shortcuts, putting these function keys again in the list will not create an accurate count of all the shortcuts.

Chapter 5: Discovering Ctrl Combinations

There are more than 50 Ctrl key combinations that you can use in the Excel sheet, with some shortcuts comprising of special characters instead of the usual alphanumeric ones. Thus, it would be unpractical to include every possible shortcut, especially if there's a little chance that a typical user will use them all. With these reasons, only the f14 most valuable Ctrl shortcuts will be contained in the list below.

Shortcut #87: Ctrl + ;
Ctrl + ; will show the current date in the active cell.

Shortcut #88: Ctrl + Shift + #
Ctrl + Shift + # will change the date into a day-month-year format.

Shortcut #89: Ctrl + A
This is an alternative to Shortcut #13: Ctrl + Shift + Spacebar. Pressing these keys will also select the whole worksheet.

Shortcut #90: Ctrl + C
Ctrl + C will copy the contents of the active cell.

Shortcut #91: Ctrl + F
If you need to search for a specific data, you don't have to go to the Home tab and choose Find & Select. By pressing Ctrl + F, you can now access the Find and Replace dialog box immediately.

Shortcut #92: Ctrl + K
To insert or edit a hyperlink, use this shortcut.

Shortcut #93: Ctrl + R
This activates the Fill Right command. To use this, simply click on a cell you want filled then press Ctrl + R. It will copy all the formatting and contents of the cell to its left.

Shortcut #94: Ctrl + S
Ctrl + S will automatically save your file in its current name, location and format.

Shortcut #95: Ctrl + V
After doing Shortcut #90: Ctrl + C, you then proceed with Ctrl + V to paste the contents that you have copied.

Shortcut #96: Ctrl + Alt + V
Since the above shortcut will paste all the data as is, the Ctrl + Alt + V will give you most pasting options as it will open the Paste Special dialog box.

Shortcut #97: Ctrl + W
This combination is an alternative to Shortcut #66: Ctrl + F4, which closes the Excel program.

Shortcut #98: Ctrl + X
This will cut the contents of an active cell. When you say "cut", it will remove the data in a cell and will place it temporarily in the Clipboard so that you can paste the contents in another cell.

Shortcut #99: Ctrl + Y
The Ctrl + Y shortcut runs the Redo function, which means that it will repeat the previous command that you have done.

Shortcut #100: Ctrl + Z
Lastly, Ctrl + Z serve as the shortcut for the Undo function. This will reverse your latest command in Excel.

And that finishes our countdown for the Top 100 keyboard shortcuts in Microsoft Excel. To wrap things up, the last chapter will provide some pointers in "memorizing" these shortcuts the easiest way.

Chapter 6: Pointers for the Excel Novice

Most people will most likely feel daunted with the mere volume of shortcuts in this book. "How can I ever memorize a hundred of these combinations?", says most people. This fear of memorization only impedes the learning process. As such, you should stay away from this negative thinking.

Practice a Couple of Shortcuts Every Week

To be able to remember these shortcuts effectively, you should use them as often as you could. Have this book by your side always so that you will have a guide as you try to absorb each of these shortcuts. Better yet, you can jot down a couple of shortcuts in a small list so that you can try some of these tricks in your school or the office.

After finishing let's say at least five shortcuts for a week, add another five in the succeeding weeks. Just don't forget the previous shortcuts that you have learned. In no time, you will be able to use these keyboard combinations without the help of a cheat sheet.

Don't Use the Numeric Keypad

Although most people on the go use laptops such as students, many people still use the full-sized keyboard that has a built-in numeric keypad at the right side.

Although several characters in the listed shortcuts are there, the Microsoft Excel does not recognize the use of numeric keypad in its shortcuts. As such, you shouldn't try to practice these shortcuts via the numeric keypad; just use the main keyboard itself.

That ends all the pointers in this guide for Excel shortcuts. With that, you should apply all the learnings that you have discovered through this book in your daily Excel tasks. Hopefully, you'll be a more efficient Excel user as you incorporate these shortcuts in using the said spreadsheet program.

Conclusion

Thank you again for purchasing this book!

I hope this book was able to help you to learn the secrets behind mastering Microsoft Excel, which are the 100 keyboard shortcuts.

The next step is to make use of these shortcuts every time you operate on the Excel application. Through this, you can now easily work on your Excel spreadsheets with only a minimal use of a mouse.

Finally, if you enjoyed this book, please take the time to share your thoughts and post a review on Amazon. We do our best to reach out to readers and provide the best value we can. Your positive review will help us achieve that. It'd be greatly appreciated!

Thank you and good luck!

Check Out My Other Books

Below you'll find some of my other popular books that are popular on Amazon and Kindle as well. Simply click on the links below to check them out. Alternatively, you can visit my author page on Amazon to see other work done by me.

C Programming Success in a Day

Android Programming in a Day

C ++ Programming Success in a Day

Python Programming in a Day

PHP Programming Professional Made Easy

HTML Professional Programming Made Easy

JavaScript Programming Made Easy

CSS Programming Professional Made Easy

Windows 8 Tips for Beginners

If the links do not work, for whatever reason, you can simply search for these titles on the Amazon website to find them.